Soil

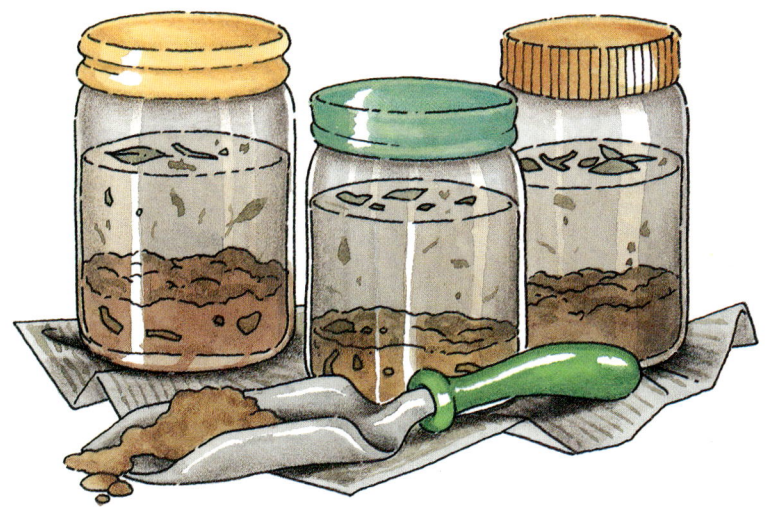

Written by Mary Ashby
Illustrated by Debbie Clark

Collins *Educational*
An imprint of HarperCollins*Publishers*

Contents

Introduction	3
What is soil?	4
Is all soil the same?	6
Why do plants need soil?	8
Why does soil need plants?	10
What animals live in the soil?	12
Conclusion	14
Glossary	16

Introduction

We all need soil.
Without soil, there would be no plants.
Without plants, people could not live.

Did you know that soil
was so important?

We can see soil in parks and gardens
and in the countryside. Even when we
cannot see it, it is still there, under
our feet.

What is soil?

Soil is a mixture of tiny parts or particles. Some soil particles come from dead plants and animals, and some come from rocks.

Try this

You will need
some dry soil
a piece of paper
a hand lens
a jar with a lid
water

1 Spread the soil out and look closely. Can you see any pieces of plants? Are there any grains of sand?

2 Put the soil in a jar of water, shake it and leave it to settle for a few hours.

3 What is floating in the water? What is at the bottom of the jar?

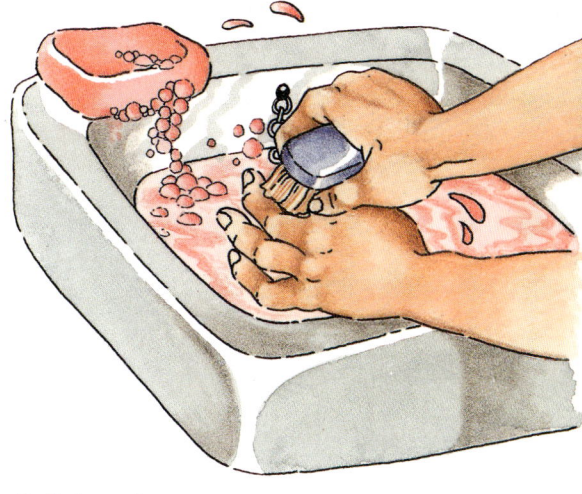

Safety note
Always remember to wash your hands when you have been touching soil.

5

Is all soil the same?

No, there are different types of soil.

Clay soil sticks together when it is wet.

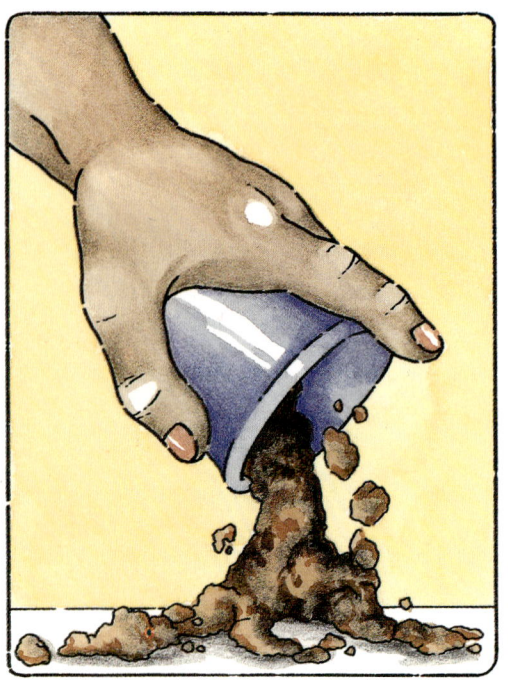

It goes hard when it is dry.

Sandy soil crumbles apart when it is wet.

Try this

You will need
soil from different places
some newspaper

1 Squeeze the soil into a ball and put it on the newspaper.

2 Does it crumble apart easily?

3 Does it stick together?

4 What kind of soil do you think it is?

Why do plants need soil?

Plants need soil for three very important reasons.

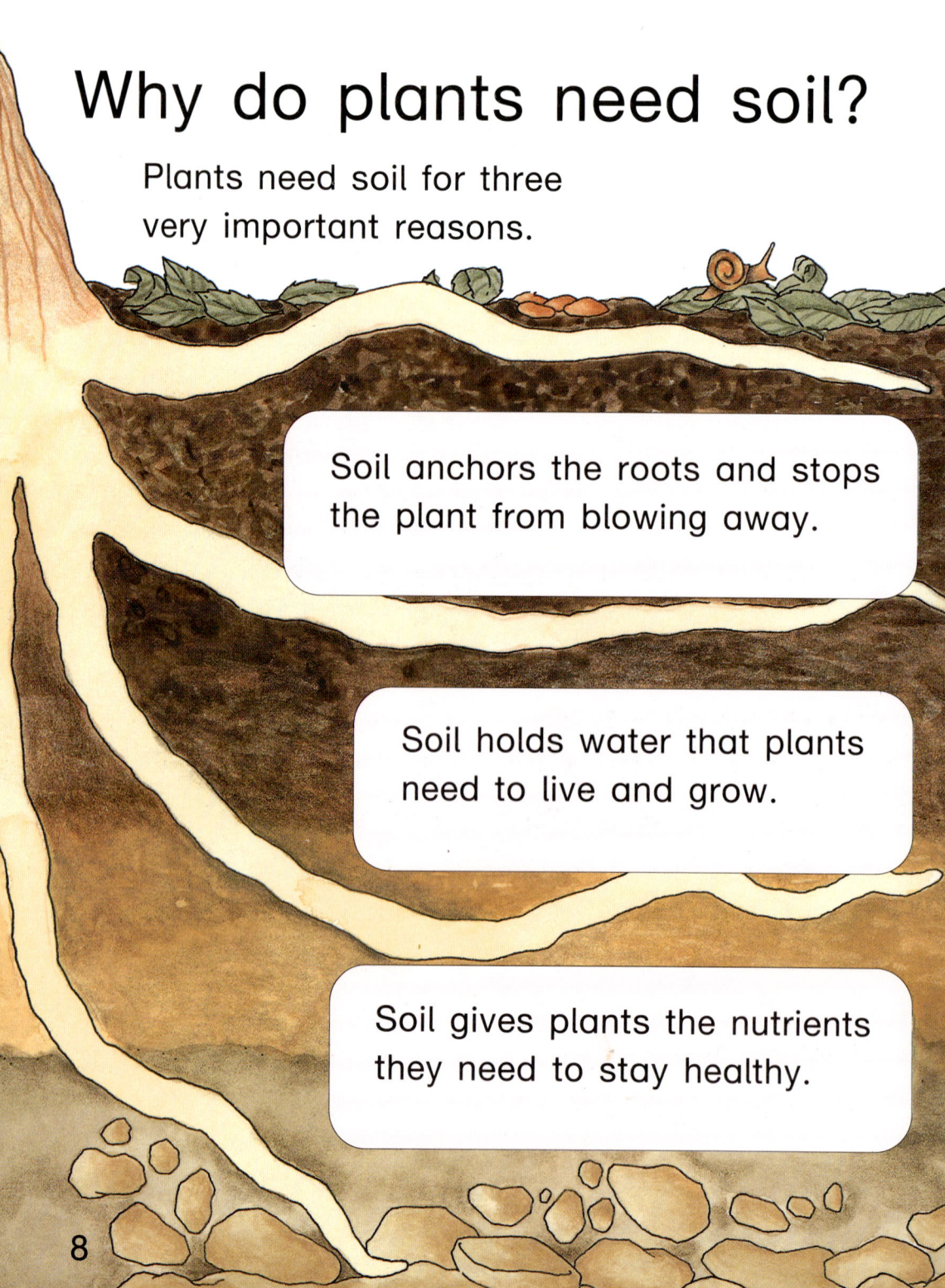

Soil anchors the roots and stops the plant from blowing away.

Soil holds water that plants need to live and grow.

Soil gives plants the nutrients they need to stay healthy.

Try this

You will need
grass seeds
three saucers
soil
sand
cotton wool
water

soil   sand   cotton wool

1 Dampen the soil, sand and cotton wool and sow some grass seeds in each saucer. Do you think all the seeds will grow?

2 Water the seeds when they get dry.

3 What differences do you notice after one week?

4 Has anything happened after two weeks?

Why does soil need plants?

Heavy rain can wash soil off the land and into rivers.

Strong winds can blow soil away.

Plant roots help to hold the soil on the land.

Try this

1 Sow grass seeds in one tray of soil and keep both trays damp.

You will need
2 trays of the same kind of soil
grass seeds
watering can
water

2 When the grass has grown, tilt the trays and water each one.

3 What happens? Does the grass help hold the soil together?

4 How could you find out if grass protects soil from the wind?

What animals live in the soil?

Rabbits and moles make burrows in the soil. Lots of very small animals live in the soil, too.

Try this

You will need a trowel a hand lens

1 Dig up some soil and look through it very carefully.

2 Can you find any of these small animals?

Conclusion

This book has told you
a little bit about soil,
and helped you to
answer some questions
for yourself.

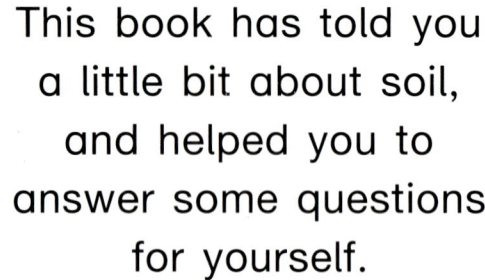

If you look in your library, you might
find other books which help you
answer more questions about soil.

Find out...

1 Why soil is different in different places.

What happens to things which are buried in the soil.

3 How we can get the soil to produce more plants.

Glossary

anchor to hold down firmly

clay sticky soil which can be used for making bricks

nutrients substances that plants need to grow and stay healthy

particles very small parts. Soil particles can be seen more clearly through a hand lens.

roots the parts of a plant that grow under the ground

sandy soil crumbly soil made mostly of sand particles